CONTENTS

BACKGROUND 1
PREFACE 2
A BRIEF HISTORY 3
LEGISLATION 4
RECENT LEGISLATION 5
THE ROMANI LANGUAGE 6
OCCUPATIONS AND EDUCATION 7
THE CULTURE OF THE TRADITIONAL GYPSY TRAVELLER COMMUNITY 8
BRICKS AND MORTAR OR A SITE 9
THE FAMILY 10
CUSTOMS OF CLEANLINESS 11
CUSTOMS OF CHASTITY 12
DEATH 13
FUNERALS 14
RELIGION 15
CONCEPTS OF JUSTICE 16
OBLIGATION TO AVOID 17
GYPSY TRAVELLERS AS CLIENTS OF THE HEALTH SERVICE 18
GOOD CARE 19
HOSPITAL 20
BIRTH 21
MATERNITY AND CHILDREN'S CLINICS 22
SCHOOL HEALTH CARE 23
AT THE DOCTOR'S 24
HOSPITAL SERVICES 25
DRESS 26
MEAL TIMES & FOOD 27
VISITS 28
A DYING PATIENT 29
GOING HOME 30
RESOURCES 31

BACKGROUND

The purpose of "An Improved Path To A Better Road" is to help health care staff and other professionals understand the Gypsy/Traveller culture. We have updated the original booklet so that it is more up to date to include recent legislation Customs are a personal thing and they may not all be followed by every Gypsy, there are variances and all cultures change and adapt over time Professional workers will most likely meet in their daily work Gypsies & Travellers who will not require any special treatment but it is useful to understand certain aspects of culture so that there are no misunderstandings

Gypsy/Traveller people only wish that their cultures are recognised and respected

There is diversity in all groups. The words Romani/Romany/Gypsy/Traveller are used interchangeably throughout the booklet. The Gypsy/Traveller communities are national minorities.

Why the need for an Information booklet?

- Derbyshire Gypsy Liaison Group (DGLG) have frequently been asked by health workers for information as there was nothing culture specific as a resource. Incidents were brought to our notice, for example:

- By a midwife who realised she had upset the family by washing her hands on the way out of the caravan in the pots bowl.

- The Environmental Health Officer who was having great difficulty in persuading a family to have a sink for 'preparing food' in the facility block in order for them to obtain their site licence.

- An old man refusing to live in a house with all the 'mucky pipes' in it but preferred to live in the garden and let his horse live in the kitchen.

- An old man refusing to get into a hospital bed, as he believed that was for the dying and he most certainly was not going to get undressed in front of young nurses.

PREFACE

The Romany people have lived in England for over 500 years and the Irish community about 150 years. There is also a Scots Gypsy tradition and this community have at last obtained recognition as an ethnic group. There is intermarriage between the groups. Society finds it difficult to understand and appreciate different cultures so information on those cultures corrects misunderstandings and helps to eradicate prejudice.

Most Gaje (non-Gypsy) people do not know much about the Romani culture although the Romani have lived in England for centuries.

Amongst Irish Traveller families you may hear words like 'buffer' or 'countryman' instead of Gaje. Gaje (gorger) means someone who is not of the Romani race and over the years has been mistakenly used to refer to people who do not travel. The aspiration to travel and to continue a nomadic way of life is paramount for Britain's Gypsies and sets them apart from many European Roma, who were forced to settle under communist regimes.

It is often difficult for the majority society to accept people who behave differently, who do not meet the 'norms' of that majority society. The strange and unfamiliar often confuse. When we speak about equality, that should not mean assimilation with out any value being placed on the distinct and varying cultures. On a daily basis professional workers meet many different kinds of people. In order for them to be able to relate to their different clients and their cultures in a positive and meaningful way, they need accurate information concerning the background of their clients. It is important to see people as a part of their family, culture and the community they live in.

There have been attempts in the past at genocide against the Romani. The latest period of persecutions occurred during World War II. At least 600,000 Roma were killed in Hitler's gas chambers. The researchers' latest estimate of the number of Roma casualties runs up to two million.

In Britain there has been documented evidence of oppression of the communities and the culture has not been valued, instead negative stereotyping has been used especially in the British press. Recent headlines of Gypsies like Stamp on the Camps Campaign and the 'land grabbing'[i] is reminiscent of the old tale of Gypsies stealing children.

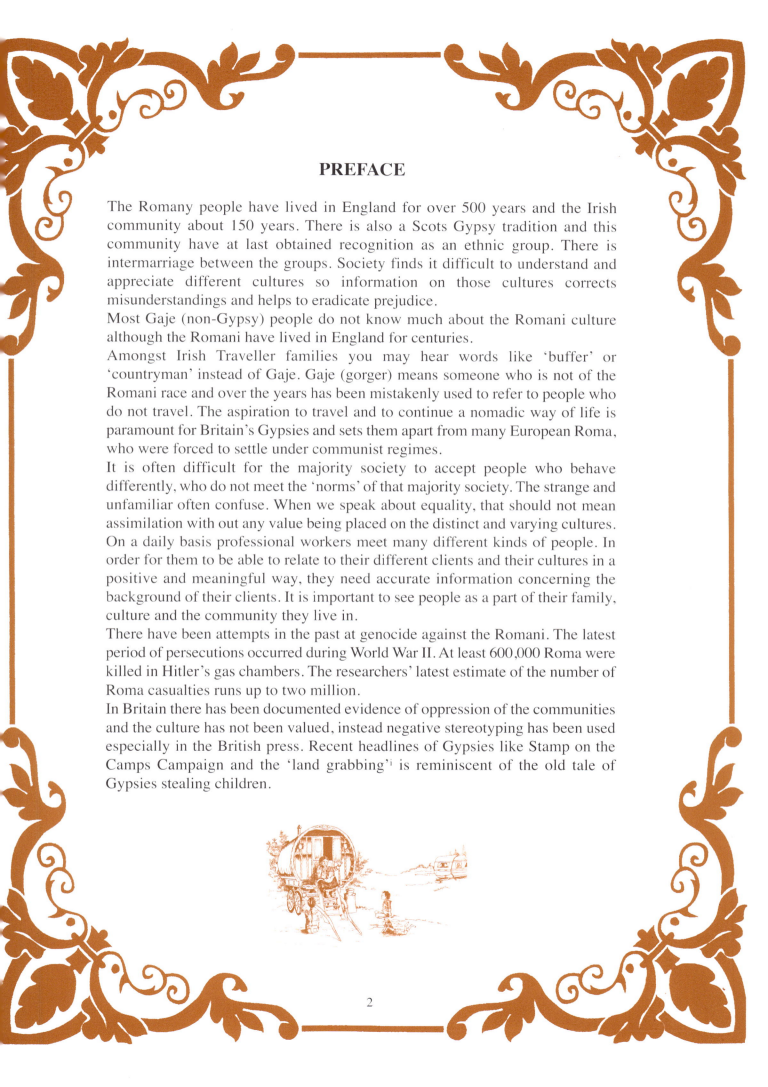

A BRIEF HISTORY

It is extremely difficult to place exact numbers of how many Traditional Travellers there are in Great Britain. Between 250,000 and 300,000 have been estimated.

The first authenticated records of their presence in Britain are in 1505 in Scotland.

The first authenticated record in England is in 1514.

Life was hard for the Gypsy people in Europe before 1500. Laws were passed to expel Gypsies from Spain and Switzerland, and by 1650 most Gypsy people were slaves.

In England under Queen Elizabeth 1, Gypsies were expelled along with all freed black slaves. Laws were passed condemning all Gypsies to death. When people were out of work, prices high and peasants were thrown off the land, it was the usual story of looking for someone to blame. Strangers make good scapegoats.

In York in 1596 magistrates made children watch while their parents were hanged just because they were Gypsies.

After 1780, anti Gypsy legislation was gradually repealed. Gypsy people became a useful source of cheap labour in the fields, blacksmiths and entertainers. Gypsies survived on the margins of society.

After the mechanisation of farming, the lifestyle of Gypsies changed drastically. Not wanted for hop or strawberry picking and other traditional trades, the people found that they had to adapt, again work was difficult to find for some families and the motorisation of families also changed the travel patterns.

The mechanisation of the traditional rural work started in the 1950s. The previous sources of livelihood did not provide sufficiently in the rural areas anymore. With industrialisation started the migration from rural areas. The changes in society were also reflected in the Roma population. Many Gypsies moved from the rural areas to the cities and towns.

Over the past decades the material well-being of some Travellers has improved but there are various issues that have been identified and need addressing, for example the unusually high mortality rate and the fact that life expectancy of Traveller men is 10 years less than the national average and 12 years less for Traveller women.

Legislation in Ireland brought about a bigger increase of Irish Travellers in England in the 1960s.

LEGISLATION

Over the years there has been a wide range of legislative measures, which have attempted to stop Romani Gypsy people and Irish Travellers from leading a nomadic way of life and therefore from actually existing. Measures date back as far as 1530, under King Henry VIII with the introduction of the "Egyptians Act", which was a ban on the immigration of Gypsies and also expelled those already in England. Queen Elizabeth brought in a further Act which states that if "the Egyptians do not give up their ungodly ways" they can be imprisoned, transported or executed.

- Highway and Byways Act 1959, which effectively criminalized the Travelling life overnight as families were not allowed to stop on the side of the road.

- The Caravan Sites and Control of Development Act of 1960. Many families who had got to know farmers over the years were displaced by this act, since farmers could no longer allow them to stay on their land, as they became eligible for fines if they technically ran a site without a valid site licence.

- The 1968 Caravan Site Act led to the creation of sites by the local authorities, but unfortunately many authorities flouted the law and did not build the sites that were needed.

- The Criminal Justice and Public Order Act 1994 swept the 1968 Caravan Sites Act away, again criminalizing this way of life. This Act also gave the Police increased powers including the right to impound vehicles if there were more than six. Guidelines issued to local authorities emphasised that before an eviction was carried out, health, educational and social needs must be taken into account.

RECENT LEGISLATION

The Race Relations Act 1976 and Race Relations (Amendment) Act 2000 will now also include Scots Gypsy Travellers. This legislation along with The Human Rights Act 1998[ii] should ensure that Romany Gypsy and Traditional Travellers are protected under the law as a minority.

It is now a statutory requirement under section 225 of the Housing Act 2004 that there should be an accommodation needs assessment of all Gypsy and Traveller people.

The Needs Assessments in some areas were very poor to start with but have improved over time. Our recommendations are that the assessments should be undertaken in a standardised way across the country in conjunction with the groups that are in the areas.

In 2006 the new planning guidance circular was issued. (Circular 01/2006 Planning For Gypsy And Traveller Caravan Sites). To a certain degree, there has been an increase in site provision through the planning system, but the majority of these are only temporary permissions whilst the new regional planning system, Regional Spatial Strategies (RSS s) gets under way. In the meantime, some districts and boroughs are objecting to providing pitches even though the identified numbers are very small compared to housing provision.

In 2007 The Showman circular was issued as many local authorities ignored the fact the Showmen should also have their needs assessed. The majority of the early assessments did not include Showmen. Showman families have a tradition of travelling and living in caravans for centuries, they have their own planning circular, Circular 04/2007 Planning For Travelling Show people (some Showmen are Romani also and some have Romani origins).

A Bill was launched by Chris Johnson (Community Law Partnership) to promote security of tenure for local authority Gypsy caravan sites. Followed by a petition in 2008. In 2008 during the Housing and Renovation Bill, the clause that made local authority sites exempt from the 1983 Mobile Homes Act was removed. At this moment in time there is consultation on some aspects of the Mobile Homes Park legislation that many felt were not appropriate for Gypsy sites. "Assignment" for example.

Community update

In 2005 The National Federation Gypsy Liaison Group formed specifically to highlight the needs of the elder Gypsy and Traveller people. It offered to host wider network meetings for the former coalition groups. Its aim is also to capacity build the communities.

NFGLG hosts a website for groups to use to put their information on and share best practice.

2009. A research document has been commissioned to look at the incidents of temporary permissions. As calculations show that the rate of permissions will not be quick enough to cover the shortfall and allow for natural growth.

THE ROMANI LANGUAGE

Romani is a member of the Indo-Aryan branch of the Indo-European family of languages. Its basis is the old Indian cult language of Sanskrit, from which also Hindi, Urdu. have evolved. Romani and Hindi are sister languages though Romani separated from the Indo-Aryan branch over two thousand years ago. In many ways it is older fashioned than the modern day Hindi. Romani is an internationally spoken language, according to various sources and is spoken by approximately 40 million people in different continents and countries over the world. In India alone there are over 20 million speakers of the Romani language. According to official sources, there are 8 million speakers of Romani in Europe and according to unofficial sources the number of speakers of Romani is 12 million.

Over the course of time the Romani language has evolved into various dialects that have been influenced by the local languages. Academics say that the basic vocabulary has stayed almost the same in various dialects. This is mainly due to the closer connections between the Roma communities of different countries. The settlements in Eastern Europe helped the language to survive as the people lived in Roma only neighbourhoods, other aspects however of Roma culture suffered.

In England the dialect is known as Romanes.

Due to the history of persecution, many older Romani Gypsies think that the least outsiders know of their customs and language the better and it was frowned on to share language and customs with outsiders. The diminished use of Romani led to a demise of the language in the 1960s and 70s The evangelist movement that swept through France in the 1970's then through Spain and Britain in the 1980's saw a revival of the language as biblical stories and bible reading groups in the Romani language grew. However changes in the Gypsy people's living conditions and rapid cultural changes have threatened the life and development of the Romani language for some groups. The Irish Traveller language has a completely different root from Romany and is not related in any way, neither is it related to Gaelic. The language is known as, Cant or Gammon. It is still regarded as quite a secret language. Over the years of contact and intermarriage between some families means that some words have crossed over from one group to another for example 'mort' both Romany Gypsy and Irish Travellers would understand this word for woman.

In recent years it has been recognised that it is useful to record and keep the language for the younger generation DVD and books record varying dialects. This is important so that the correct form of word is used and passed on. Some words in the language are used only by certain families, some are regional for example 'gavver' is used in the south for policeman but not in the north.

OCCUPATIONS AND EDUCATION

Years ago the differences between agricultural or land workers and Gypsy Travellers were not big. Education was valued by neither group because crafts were passed from father to son and mother to daughter. The difference in the level of education increased with industrialisation and progress.

Traditionally Gypsy men worked in tasks associated with horse-trading and horse handling although, some of course worked in other trades. Summertime and autumn meant work in agriculture and the fields. They undertook barn building, barn spraying; they harvested crops and laid hedges. Women sold things from door to door, hawking (or knocking). The whole family took part in earning the living. Families moved from one village to another. They liked their own autonomy and independence. Gypsy men like to be their own boss. This is also true of the Roma community. The peddlers certificate is a means of registering a door to door seller and permits them to work in that area. They are issued by the local police. One of the problems with a peddlers certificate (Hawkers licence) is that you have to be resident in the area for 6 weeks or more before applying for one. This wasn't much of a problem years ago when you could stay anywhere for a few weeks. Nowadays however, with legislation changing, they have become increasingly difficult to obtain.

Industrialisation has made the traditional occupations of Travellers unprofitable and new occupations had to be found. Gypsy Traveller people have always been able to adapt. Erstwhile dealers in all manner of new and second-hand goods have now become experts in other fields. Many families have landscape businesses, lay paving and build conservatories. Others are involved in such trades as thatching and stone walling. Some schemes for adult education have offered a chance to modernise traditional skills to meet modern needs, but there is little joined up thinking across Great Britain as a whole, and more could be done in some areas. The traditional occupations have laid a good basis for new occupations like selling used cars instead of horse trading, retailing commodities for starting a small business, the traditional women's skills for working as a dressmaker or seamstress. Horse racing and harness racing has provided a livelihood for some in various occupations relating to the raising and training of the horses. Boxing is also popular as a skill to earn money. Traditional Travellers, both Romany and Irish are reserved toward education since school had been seen as a means to assimilate Gypsy Travellers into the majority. The attitude toward education has changed during the last few years to a positive direction regarding the fact that the majority would like to see the children go through primary school. There is not a big uptake on secondary level school, however early apprentice schemes seem to be popular with the traditional fairground community and may be picked up in the future by other traditional Travellers. There have been successful long distance learning programs with lap tops amongst the Gypsy and Showman population.

THE CULTURE OF THE TRADITIONAL TRAVELLER COMMUNITY

In today's world it is the positive aspects of Gypsy culture that need to be pointed out. Those of close family ties and traditional values. It is very easy to pick out health problems and relate them to culture rather than to relate them to the fact that the majority do not want to accept the minority culture. We all need a safe base from which to fight our corner. A safe base for Britain's Gypsy/Traveller mainly consists of a trailer (Living caravan) and somewhere to park it. It has been accepted in UK law that there is a cultural aversion built up over the centuries within the Gypsy psyche with regard to bricks and mortar (Conventional housing), this needs to be recognised and catered for to alleviate the potential of mental health problems for the community. It is a recognised fact that a Romany Gypsy that has for varying reasons moved into or, spent a number of years in an house can be suffering silently. There have been cases where elder relatives have moved back, out of housing and returned to the piece of land where their family may have a short-term planning permission to stay. This suffering is compounded by the 'gypsy' (Note the small g) status requirement in planning law. If the elder is not found to have a nomadic habit of life (After 25 or 30 yrs of living in a house) difficulties will arise. They can be, regardless of circumstance or ethnic ties to the road as a Romany Gypsy, found not to be a 'gypsy' for the purposes of planning law.

This is hurtful, discrimatory and is considered by the main Romany Gypsy/Traveller groups to be a form of legislative genocide. It goes against the Chapman v UK [2004] European Court of Human Rights ruling that the UK should facilitate the Gypsy way of life (note capital G). It also is contrary to European legislation. The Framework Convention for the Protection of National Minorities[iv].

DGLG presented a petition in the House of parliament in 2004. The National Federation of Gypsy Liaison Groups re launched this again in 2009.

BRICKS AND MORTAR OR A SITE

Many traditional families have an aversion to bricks and mortar and become increasingly depressed when forced, (due in the main to the lack of sites and occasionally to ill health) to resort to living in a house.

There is an increasing suicide rate amongst Travellers because of this phenomenon.

In R (Margaret Price v Carmarthenshire CC [2003] the judge recognised this phenomenon and stated that to many Gypsy families the thought of going into housing would be like living in a "rat infested barn"

Increasingly, because of the lack of sites, many families have sought to make their own provision by buying land on which to place their caravans, and to apply for planning permission for their own family. This is because they want to remain living in the manner to which they were born and did not choose. Due to extensive lobbying by DGLG and other Gypsy/Traveller groups, the 1/94 guidance planning circular was put in place not long after the abolition of the 1968 Caravan Sites Act. However, over 90% of planning applications by Gypsy families were turned down under this circular, as they fall into a "catch 22" in the planning laws. Many families are developing stress-related illnesses and nervous disorders.

The increase in stress related illness could be linked directly to the problems of the family not having a safe base to place their home.

For some Travellers living in a house, everyday life may have become easier, but new problems arise which outsiders often find difficult to understand or accept without knowing the reasons behind the problems. For example, when a member of the family dies, some families will want to move as soon as possible. Assigning new housing may be necessary even if the person did not die in the residence, because some families will move out regardless. The customs and practices of Romani families vary from one to another. How each family follows the traditions should be born in mind and discussed separately. Many housed Gypsy/Travellers suffer from racist incidents, causing them to retreat further into isolation or suddenly go back onto the road with no authorised place to stop.

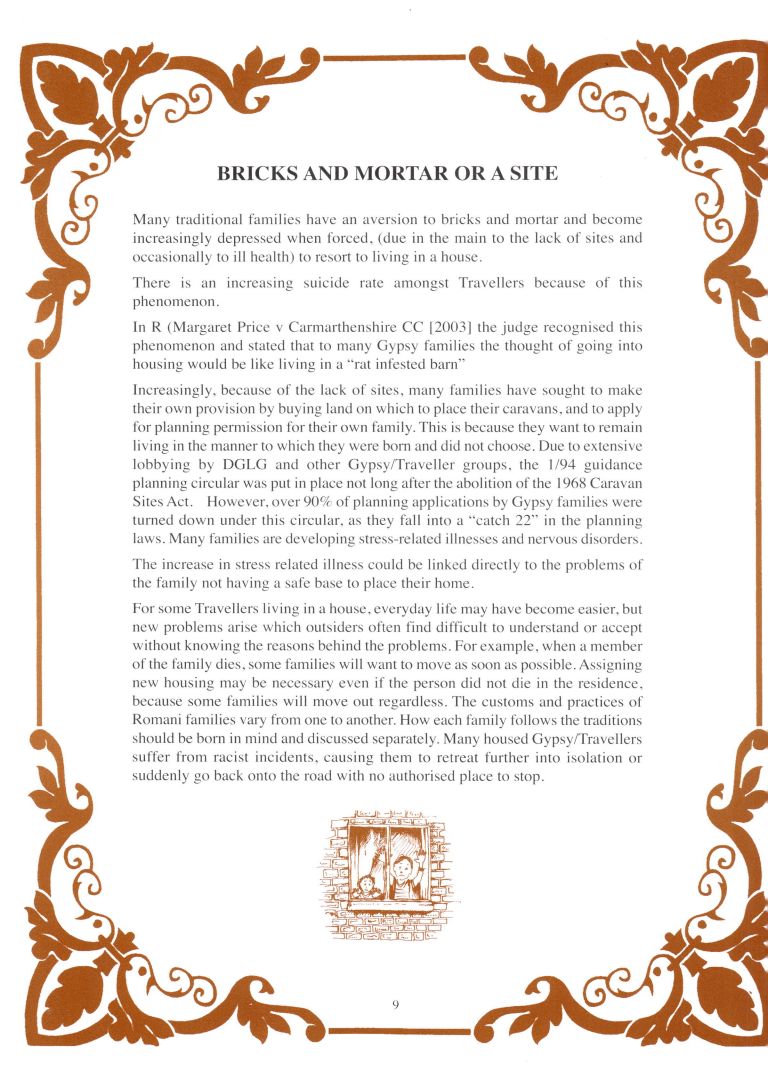

THE FAMILY

Family is extremely important. If a relative is having hard times then the rest of the family tries to help and provide support. The man is seen as the head of the family and the woman very much the heart of it. There is no conflict, it is well balanced. Both are important for the well being of the family. A man is appreciated according to how well he can support his family and a woman according to how well she manages the home and the children. Many people on the outside consider this aspect very old fashioned, and very often think that women are kept down, but in reality the situation works well for most families. As can be seen in recent years, Gypsy women like Sylvie Dunn and Kay Beard of the UK Association of Gypsy Women have been at the forefront of politics. Likewise, Maggie Smith Bendell who has taken on the planning system for many, many families.

Women like these above are fundamentally strong people. Although Romani women still have many responsibilities, they do not feel oppressed. The question of equality between men and women is not seen as important. Men and women share balanced roles and in days gone by if a woman was a particularly good hawker selling door to door, a stew would be on the fire when she got home. The men are in the background when issues connected with the role of women (Especially those subjects to do with health) are dealt with, and vice versa. By the same token, a woman would not interrupt her husband while he was discussing a deal.

It is important to note that the differences in the roles of men and women can allow some men to discriminate and treat their wives and family badly. This is not due to Romani/Traveller culture and it should not be seen as part of that culture, but rather as an excuse. In truth, it is usually due to problems within the family.

The decreasing role of men as the head of the family is visible in the modern day development of society and families. Traveller women have always worked outside the home to provide for the family, whether due to hawking, fruit picking or part time work. Therefore, on the whole it has been easier for the women to re-educate themselves, keep up to date with modern issues, and to find their place in the labour market. It is important to acknowledge that vocational work should be valued. There is almost a disregard for hard manual labour and the work of a pair of hands in today's age, is not valued. We are in the days of the insurance broker, the banker, and the computer expert. For families whose trade has practiced by generations of men, life is tough. Further compounded by no knocking/hawking signs. It is important to assist men in such things as chain saw safety certificates. If you do not have certain certificates you cannot hire a chainsaw for example.

Elders are respected in the Gypsy and Traveller communities; both genders are responsible for the well being of elders and children. It is typical for all the members of the Romani community to take part in the upbringing of the children and to pass on traditions. Parents pass on their skills, trades and professions to their offspring.

How much a child learns in school, or how skilled he/she might become is not primarily important to Traveller parents. The most important thing is for children to have a safe and happy childhood. Parents will try to protect their children from the harm that they themselves may have suffered. Some parents have bad memories of how they were treated in school and would not want that for their own children. Gypsy/Traveller children are brought up with responsibilities and are independent at quite an early age. It is not unusual for an 11 or 12 year old girl to be adept at making the family meal if need be. The children, like their parents, have to be resilient. Otherwise, the negative attitude of the outside world would get them down. An enhanced sense of community gives the children strong roots and a good start. Many families can trace their families back 400 years + the branches of many family trees overlapping. A family can have three family photographs that span 11 generations for example.

Gypsies/Travellers have not placed their children in day-care until quite recently.

CUSTOMS OF CLEANLINESS
(Mochadi)

There are very many customs amongst Gypsy people concerning cleanliness and chastity. Cleanliness is very important, it stands to reason that being in a small living space there needs to be strict rules in place to ensure good health, however, many cleanliness beliefs are also of a cultural ceremonial nature. These beliefs are seen daily, they include all activities from handling the dishes, cutlery and food to washing the laundry, from clothing to the relationship between the generations

Some examples are, for instance, food dishes and cutlery are never placed where one would sit, stand or walk. Cloths and kitchen towels are not used for any other purpose and would not be used to wipe down furniture. Dishcloths, kitchen towels and tablecloths are washed in a separate washbowl. Some families may wash the clothes of younger men and women separately. Underwear would never be washed with tea towels

Washing hands is very important. Prior to preparing food or dishes hands are washed. Food bags will be put directly on to a higher surface or table, never on the floor. The things that can be occasionally on the floor, such as handbags and toys, are never put on the table. Even very young children know that feet and things on the floor must never be put on the table. The household pets have their own dishes that are not washed in the family pots bowl. Allowing dogs to eat from family plates is abhorrent.

The life of Gypsy/Traveller people has changed remarkably over the last twenty years. Some of the customs of cleanliness have been watered down and some others are not in use anymore, but it does help to be aware of the concepts. If one thinks of the Kosher law within the Jewish community, mochadi is similar. For example, one could have bought a brand new expensive cut glass fruit bowl, but if someone is sick in it, the bowl then becomes mochadi, and no amount of washing will make it clean enough again in which to place fruit. There are some very traditional families out there that do follow some of the older forms of mochadi lore.

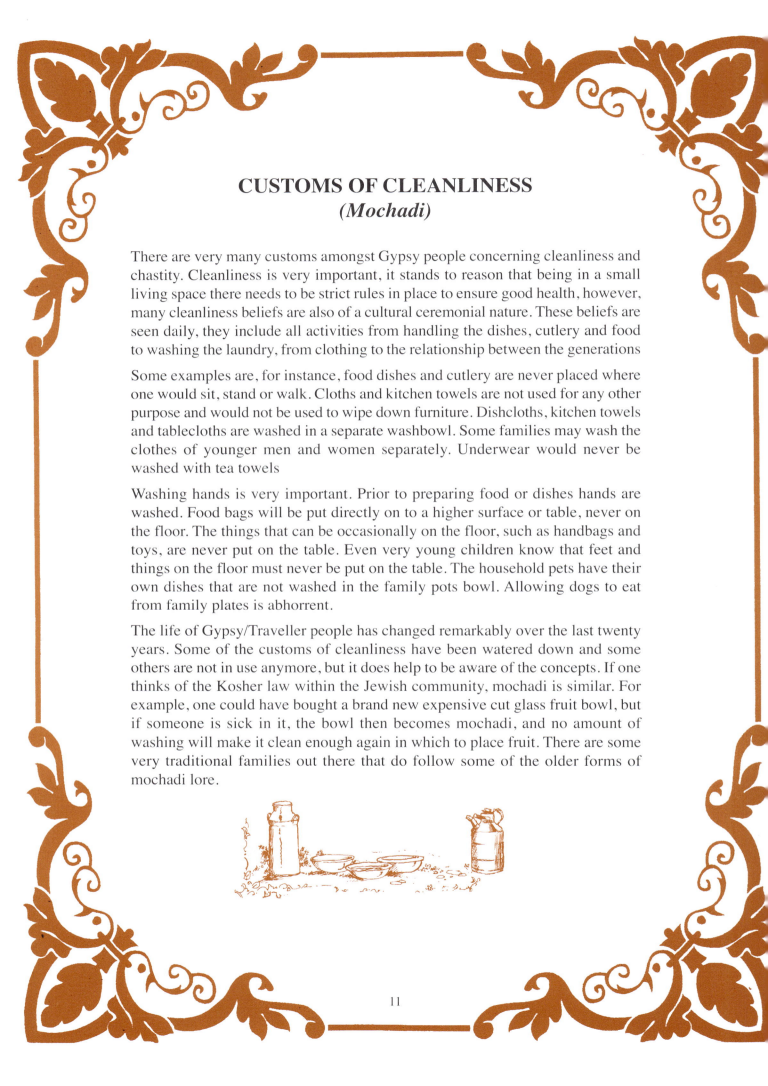

CUSTOMS OF CHASTITY

- Traditional Travellers have very traditional values and one of the reasons many will not send their children to secondary school is because of sex education. The Romani community and Irish Travellers of different generations do not discuss sexual issues. Gypsy/Travellers have a bashful attitude toward sexuality. Many parents do not know that they can arrange that their child does not receive Personal and Social Education at school. Schools need to understand that morals are not to be weakened in any way and it is not their role to discuss these issues with Gypsy youngsters.

- A pregnancy or any other aspect regarding women's health is not discussed in the presence of men. This subject is considered woman's business. Many a health visitor or midwife laments Gypsy men running in the opposite direction as they approach!

- Pregnancy used to be hidden for as long as possible. Big scarves and loose clothing were used to almost hide the pregnancy, especially if other small children were in the family. This did not mean that children were unwelcome. Gypsies/ Travellers love their children and grandchildren but it was not considered good manners at one time to bring the subject up even if it was very obvious that a baby was on the way. Nowadays fashions have changed. Some families are not so coy and grannies lament with the fact that they went "to bed with more on than some of the young lasses go out in today!"

- The concept of mochadi needs to be taken into account at the time of birth for families - again, this is similar to the Jewish belief and also concerning the time of month for women. This is a subject for women only. It was at one time (and it still is) for some families considered mochadi to touch meat at this time or to handle food and cook.

DEATH

A death is experienced strongly and deeply and there are many traditions concerning death. Memories can be so strong that a family find it difficult to live in the same place where the deceased lived with them. Traditionally families always move off a piece of land where they have been stopping when a death occurs. The family will move to another place after the funeral. All personal belongings such as clothes of the deceased are burnt. Other Gypsy Travellers will not want them. Some families do express fears of ghosts and like to follow these traditions. At one time it was not considered good manners to bring the subject of a dead relative up unless the family started talking about them first.

Gold & jewellery is kept and handed down as inheritance and as family mementos. In years gone by it was traditional to bury the deceased with their gold and jewellery. Photos of the deceased are very important memorabilia and they are carefully stored and passed on. Some families have lost family photographs through caravan fires and this causes some anguish. It is not unusual for family documents to be burnt accidentally during funeral times

If the deceased owned property there will be no inheritance arguments. It is considered very bad to fall out at times of a death and especially if the subject is about inheritance. In most cases the deceased has named the person who will inherit. The oldest son may have some privileges as is the tradition in a lot of cultures but in general all children are treated equally.

An elder woman once had some money taken from her mistakenly in a police raid, her husband had left it to her wrapped in a bag, she was distraught that when it was returned to her it was not that particular bundle that she had originally been given. It was not the same to her.

FUNERAL TIME

Funeral arrangements will be taken care of by close family. Invitations to funerals are not usually sent out, but everyone to whom the deceased has been important will come to the funeral. Friends also of the close relatives might also attend.

Everyone will come to the caravan or the home of the family of the deceased the night before the funeral. It is traditional to 'sit up' so the close relatives and friends of the deceased will stay awake for that night. (Some families sit up for more than one night). The elderly and the children will go to bed when they get tired. No one 'must' stay awake but usually at least some close relatives will stay awake throughout the night. The deceased will be remembered during the night and devotions held. This is the last night on earth and the following day he or she will be buried. Therefore the loss will be experienced as final during the night. It is not popular to cremate the body within the Gypsy tradition although that is not unheard of occasionally. Before the funeral photos of close relatives or other mementoes will be put inside the coffin.

At this time, men will gather in a separate caravan to that of the women. A fire is lit for the duration of sitting up time.

There can be a short quiet time in the chapel but the actual funeral service often is held next to the grave. The priest will hold the service according to the regular liturgy. Hymns are often avoided, as most of the congregation would not be able to sing from the sheet, literacy being a problem. Some families get round this by hiring a choir. At one time men would congregate on one side of the church and women on the other for any service. A meal will be served before the funeral guests return to their homes. Some families, especially older Gypsy Travellers, will not eat meat at funerals.

There will be members of the family to support relatives until the funeral. Right after the funeral and the family members have departed, the loss will be experienced quite strongly. Therefore others will visit regularly for a while.

Taking care of the grave is considered to be very important. The family usually visit the grave regularly to commemorate occasions like birthdays, Christmas, Easter etc to bring flowers and to keep the grave tidy. Great care is taken not to tread on the head of the grave. The first anniversary to the grave is very important and the stationing of the memorial stone.

RELIGION

For the most part, many Romani and Irish Travellers have adopted the religion of their country of residence and have always accepted a belief in God. They cover many denominations including the Christian Spiritualist church and Jehovah's Witnesses. Recently, many have joined the Born Again Christian Church and it is not uncommon if someone dies for the *sitting up* (see page 14) to be held at the church, especially if the family now live in a house. Irish Travellers are traditionally Catholic. Some Irish Traveller and Romani families have inter-married now and therefore one cannot assume which denomination a Traveller follows. Faith does not interfere with cultural beliefs and faith is seen as a personal subject.

CONCEPTS OF JUSTICE

A certain system of norms of justice based on the community's inner views can be found in any community. Traditional Travellers also have their norms of justice and morality a lot of this is based on cultural belief and some things that are considered very shocking to the Gypsy community are deemed less shocking to the community outside. Bad behaviour within the community is addressed within the community and the person who is found guilty of misconduct will receive a punishment decided by the community. Mostly the punishment is moral, a certain type of a loss of reputation. At times a form of excommunication takes place especially if the offender has for example hurt a child or caused harm to an elder person. To some this may seem as a petty punishment but in reality it works very effectively. In the Romani community, the concept of honour toward other Romani is important. Misconduct can mean that close relatives can also be hurt by their actions. This can be seen working when a whole family may suddenly leave a site even if they have had to wait a considerable number of years to get onto the site. An incident can be 'shaming' and a person can be put into 'shame'

Some of the fights between both Romani and Irish Travellers have been labelled publicly as feuding. This view is very misleading. There can be some strong cultural belief behind the headline. The avoidance and yielding mechanism has traditionally been in place among Gypsies & Travellers for an eternity. If serious damage has been caused to the other person, the family take all possible measures to avoid the persons who caused the problem. An incident can be passed down through the generations; some feuds are lost to memory, why they started and why they remain.

At times the traditional Traveller community have felt that they cannot approach the usual justice systems and this has been due to a lack of trust through the years. Nowadays there is a move to change that belief. Since the McPherson report on Stephen Lawrence, Gypsy people need to be a part of Police training in their ethnic and diversity issues.

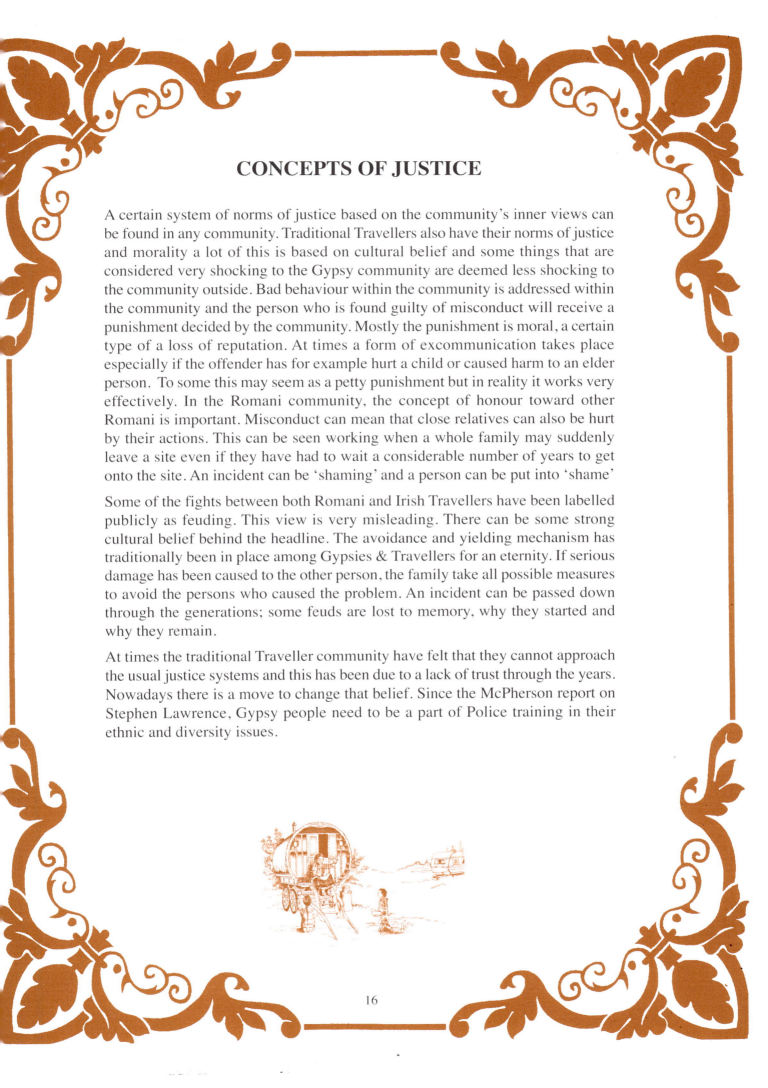

OBLIGATIONS TO AVOID

In sites and housing, the concepts of what is right is important if something bad has happened between families. For example, if one Traveller has committed a serious crime against another, the family and close relations of the culprit will have to move to another place. The guilty person and his/her relations need to avoid the family and close relations of the family affected. Because the Romani community is relatively small and the families know one another, it would be too painful to be in daily contact. A sorrow caused by someone you know is even harder to bear than if a stranger caused it. Therefore Romani families have a mechanism of avoidance and yielding. To some people this may seem unreasonable. It may be easier to understand this if one thinks of the situation where one's neighbour would have killed a member of his/her family. It would surely be painful to see that person every day. Seeing him/her would open the wounds caused by the loss over and over again. It is easier to move on and try and ignore the situation so that one does not have to deal with those who have caused the suffering. It also means that there may be family feud avoided.

At times there have been difficulties with site managers and housing authorities who don't understand the above reasons, since Travellers don't openly discuss always things of this nature due to custom. Little by little the authorities have got more information and have been able to consider the Romani/Traveller customs during the allocation process for example, of site pitch or house. It is crucial that the site manager should have essential knowledge of the community and their word as to who pulls onto a site must be taken into account and be final.

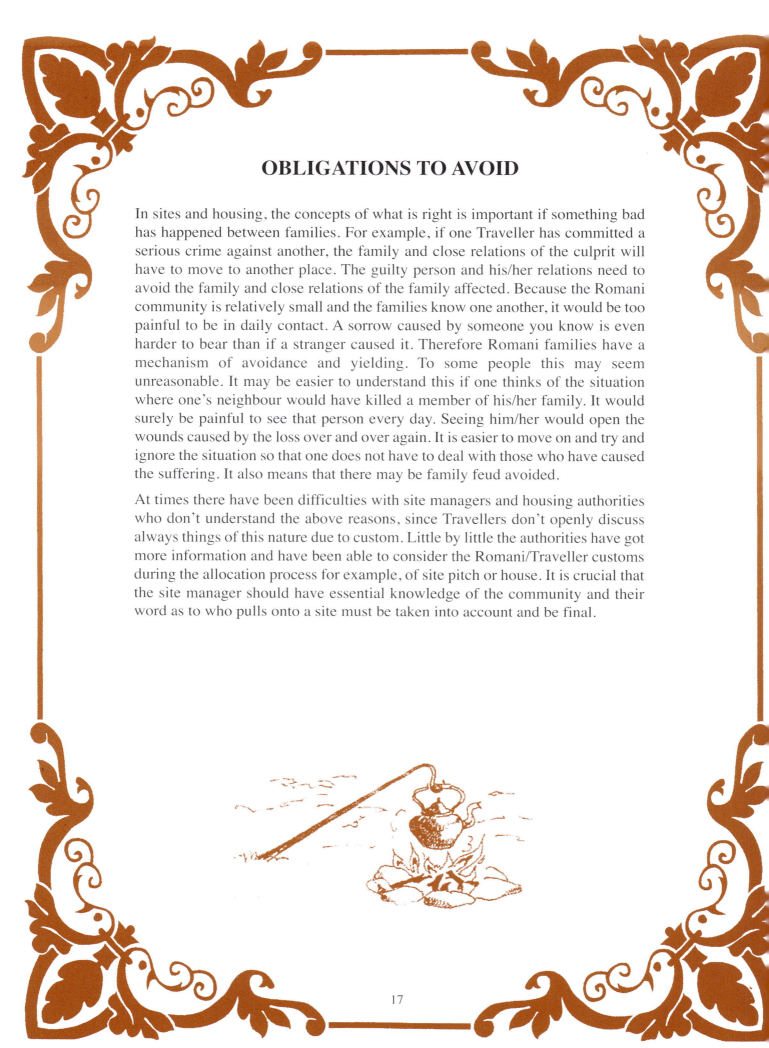

GYPSY TRAVELLERS AS CLIENTS OF THE HEALTH SERVICE

Social conditions and poor health are directly related. Lack of sites with adequate facilities and poor housing conditions take their toll on the health of the middle and older generations.

In the Gypsy/Traveller culture there are various ways to support those who have fallen ill and their close relatives. Support decreases the amount of worry and concern. Building a safe atmosphere helps recovery. In general a family will take care of ill and disabled members. They are not placed in institutions willingly. In recent times a "care home" has had to be found for those older Travellers who could not travel anymore and suffer, for example, from Alzheimer's disease.

Traditionally it was and is still not uncommon for an unmarried daughter to be the one who looked after elderly parents.

When Travellers were based more in the rural areas, the use of medicinal plants was common, as it was very important to avoid all contagious diseases while travelling. Cleanliness and hygiene were strictly enforced. Those who were gravely ill had their own dishes, which were washed apart from all the others and, when they were not needed anymore, were thrown away. The bedding of the ill person was carefully kept apart from other people's bedding, changed often and boiled when washed. The washing of hands has played an important role in infection prevention. Many families still hold onto these customs.

There is evidence to show a high suicide rate amongst the Traveller community. Usually Travellers are more accepting of mental illnesses than the gaje community. Those who suffer from mental illnesses may find them a hard burden. The meeting of two quite different cultures can become a problem in psychiatric treatment. The person's alienation from their social and cultural community is often behind their mental illness. Many of the people who have fallen between two cultures are unable to identify themselves with either culture and suffer mentally. The early care of a disabled person should receive special attention in health care. Some parents who look after their disabled child at home may not know how to give the child enough stimulation the parents should be encouraged and given information about the importance of special education that is available. Traditionally families do not agree with segregating children with a disability and institutionalising them away from their family.

There is evidence to show that the neo-natal death rate is nearly four times higher than the national average.

GOOD CARE

- To Gypsy/Travellers, a good health worker is one that is professional, co-operative and friendly. A positive attitude is always important and an interest in family wellbeing is essential. The health visitor usually has a good relationship with Gypsy /Traveller people on sites.

- Many families consider health visitors good friends and over the years many have become a strong link between the communities.

- Lack of knowledge means that many health workers feel afraid or wary to approach a Traveller patient and Gypsy/Traveller people hope that their cultural background is taken into consideration in the care that they may need. In order to be able to fulfil this wish the health worker needs the correct information to help build a positive relationship with the patient.

- Information on ethnic minorities should be included in the training of health care staff. Aspects of Romani/Traveller culture should be discussed within the training, using suitable connections.

- The cleanliness and chastity customs of the Romani culture as well as the importance of extended family can cause many problems and confusion. Many hospitals have been able to recognise and respect the customs and practices of the Romani/Traveller people after receiving information on the Romani Gypsy & Traveller cultures. Hospitals can work with families with respect and flexiblity.

- Discussion with the patient is always the important factor because it is the best way to avoid confusion. If you do not know something, don't be afraid to ask. If the carer or health worker notices that the patient appears distressed about something, he/she should encourage the patient to talk about it. It may be something really simple but is worrying the patient culturally.

- Health visitors should not feel that they need to be accompanied by the police if they visit sites. Most have built up relationships with families but sometimes sites are run badly and there are problems because of this factor.

HOSPITAL

Many Gypsy/Travellers in the past have used the Accident and Emergency department as a means to access health care. Sometimes this has been because the family has been unable to access health care through a local Doctor's surgery, or through a lack of knowledge of the services in that area. In addition some practices have refused to register Gypsy families. On the plus side, some hospitals now undertake diversity training. However, there is a need to undertake more work as Britain is a very multicultural society. Same sex wards are frowned upon and refused. Most of the population do not like the idea of mixed wards and feedback has confirmed that this practice is to be stopped within the hospital system.

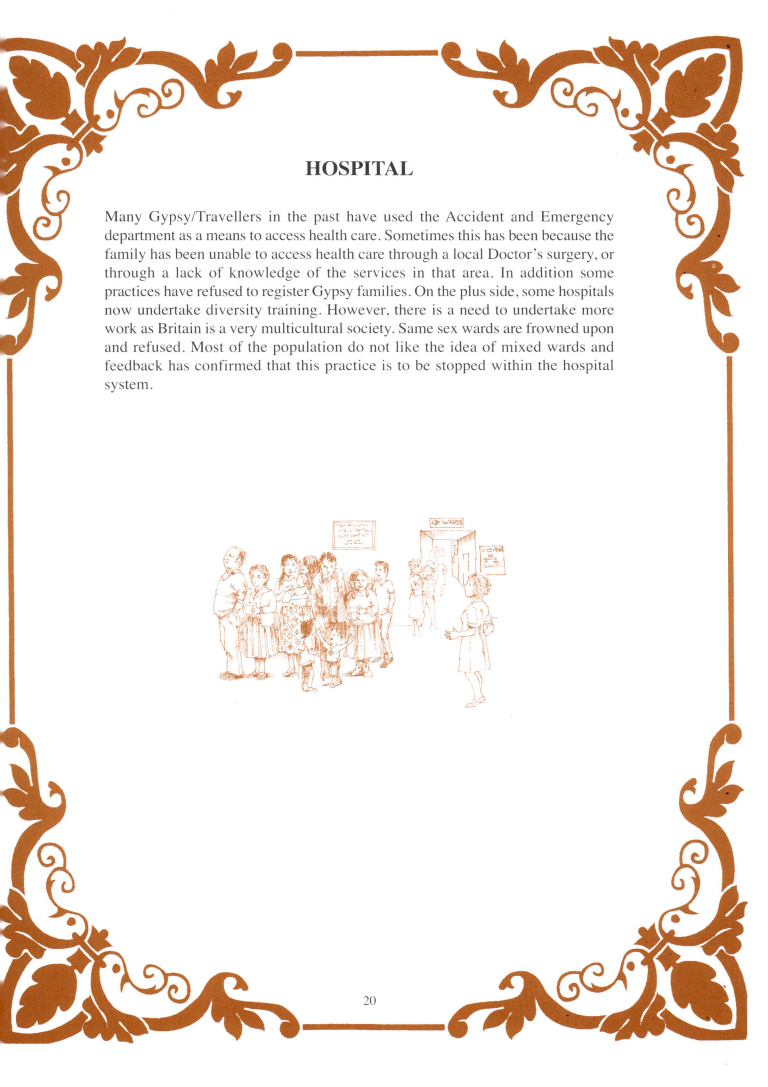

GIVING BIRTH

Traditionally Gypsy/Traveller fathers do not attend the actual birth of a baby. The young father-to-be stays with his wife until the baby is about to be born and then comes away, the prospective grandmother taking his place. Nowadays the father is welcomed in the delivery suite by his wife but the older generation still frown on this and wonder at why men would want to get involved with what is essentially 'women's' business

Since many Traveller mothers will try to leave the hospital to go home with the baby as soon as possible after labour, the hospital staff should advise them of the risks that relate to going home too early. At the same time the fact that the mother needs time to recover in peace should be also highlighted.

It was common that when the mother and baby came home from the hospital she was not allowed to do the household chores for a few weeks.

In some families it would be viewed as mochadi for her to be preparing food, not as common now as it was but there needs to be an awareness of this. Some Roma believe in this strongly today. The mother always had a 'helper', usually another family member or friend who took care of the kitchen duties and looked after hers. In many families this custom is still followed. The child is never breast-fed in front of strangers. Aftercare is best not discussed in 'mixed company' (women and men).

Don't worry if the men disappear when the health visitor/midwife visit, this is a woman's subject only.

The older generation still expect the new mother to be 'churched' before she crosses her own threshold or anyone else's. Churched means to go to church and give thanks to God for your child and its safe delivery. A priest or a clergyman from your chosen faith has to 'church' you. This is seen as a ritual cleansing as well as thanks to God. Some Gypsy/Travellers will refuse food or drink from a young mother who has not been churched. This can be classed as an old fashioned custom but some families still adhere to it.

MATERNITY AND CHILDREN'S CLINICS

- Gypsy/Travellers use health clinic services less than members of the non-travelling community. The new walk-in clinics will be really good for the Traveller community who do have problems accessing services.

- Many Gypsy/Travellers traditionally do not use pre natal clinic services at an early stage because they do not realise and understand what they can be screened for. Some will find it difficult to attend regular appointments.

- A pregnant Gypsy/Traveller mother may register at the antenatal clinic, but unless she has pains or other needs she will not always come to the clinic regularly. She may contact the clinic near the end of her pregnancy. It is really important to promote the use of the pre-natal clinic at an early stage.

- A mother may come to the clinic with all her children, hoping they will all be checked and cared for at the same appointment.

- The agreed appointments might not be kept, in which case another appointment should be made.

- The children's clinic should take care of the regular vaccinations for the Traveller children if this is required. Bear in mind that traditionally many Gypsy people felt that vaccination was something to be wary of as you were polluting the inner body, but there is an increased understanding of vaccination. Many mothers do not like the idea of the triple vaccinations and some would prefer that these be given separately. Some mothers will pay privately for this, rather than worry about their baby having a bad reaction.

- It is always useful to obtain a mobile number, if you can, to remind people of appointments.

- There are many reasons that appointments are missed but the main one can be due to eviction. Evictions should not take place before health, educational and social assessments have been completed. All needs should be identified and addressed for Gypsy/Travellers stopping on land owned by District or Borough Councils or the County Council.

This is a requirement by law.

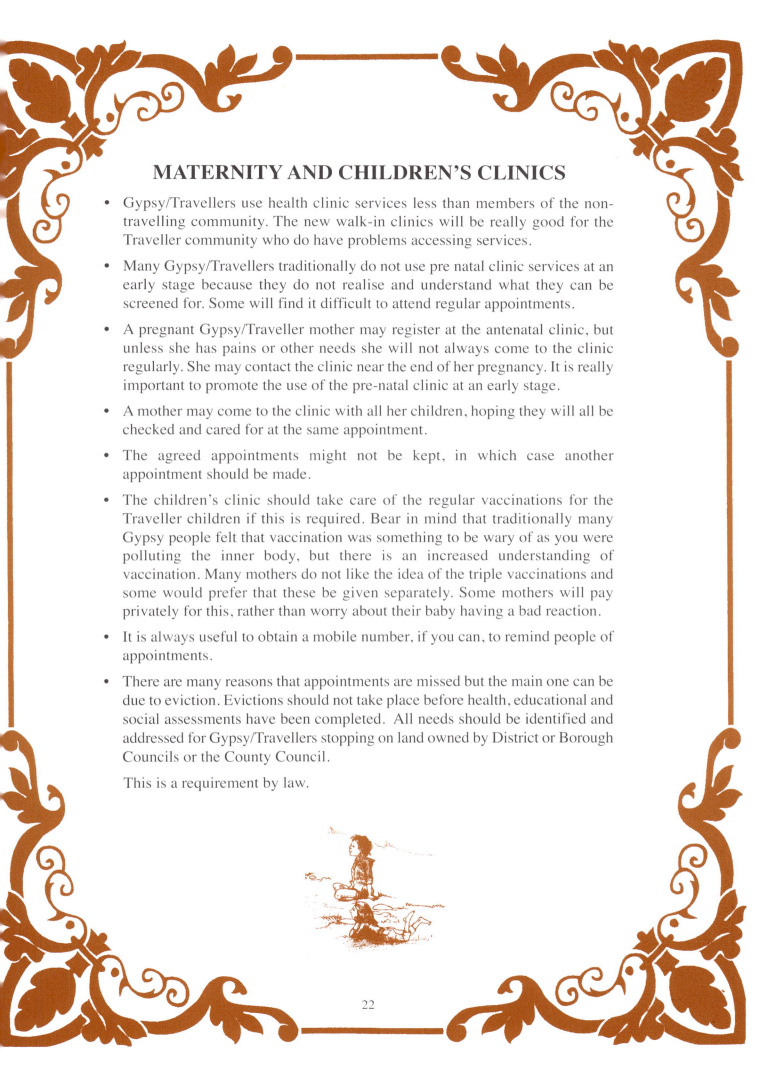

SCHOOL HEALTH CARE

- The younger Gypsy/Travellers do not discuss issues relating to gender and sexuality with the older generation.

- Even nowadays many young Travellers do not get information on puberty, contraception and pregnancy from their parents.

- Families are not in agreement with sex education in schools and do not consider it appropriate.

- Some problems may occur in physical education classes where young Traveller people do not feel comfortable wearing the gymnastics outfit or getting changed in front of strangers. Even if the parents do not insist that youngsters at this stage dress or behave according to cultural customs the young start to identify at an early age. The young may be unable or too embarrassed to tell the real reason to the teacher.

- The young may not understand that even when they are embarrassed to appear scantily clad in front of other Travellers, they do not need to be embarrassed in front of adults

- The school nurse can act as a mediator between the teacher and the young Gypsy/Travellers during any difficulties that there may be regarding cultural issues.

- Due to recent incidents in the press, many families do not allow children on school trips for fear of bad influence or something bad happening.

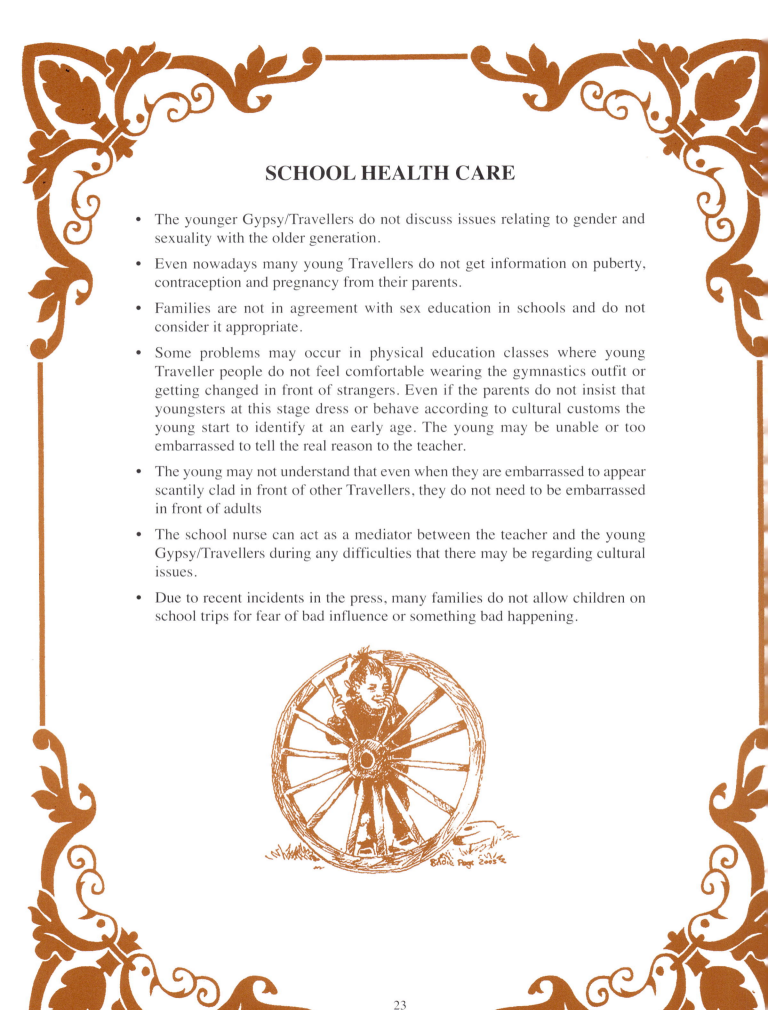

AT THE DOCTOR'S

- It would be good to emphasise at the same time that even though appointments are meant to be kept, many Travellers have difficulty keeping an appointment for differing reasons. For example, not keeping a diary or literacy problems or a sudden eviction. Some clinics will ring as a reminder.

- Many Travellers do not feel comfortable in going to the doctor's surgery alone. It is quite usual for an escort to accompany someone to hospital by sometimes four or five family members even more if the situation is a serious one

- A thorough explanation of how to take the prescribed drugs should be given. Experience has shown that some Gypsy/Travellers, especially the older ones, do not take their medication regularly or take the prescribed dosage. Some may stop taking the medicine as soon as the symptoms disappear. Some may use expired medication and even drugs prescribed to another person.

- An idea that may help the Gypsy or Traveller community would be a hand held record card. DGLG tried this in Derbyshire in the late nineties, but some GPs were reluctant to use it for fear of them being inadvertently lost. However now that we are in the time of the computer, it may be that a swipe card would be the answer to secure data protection.

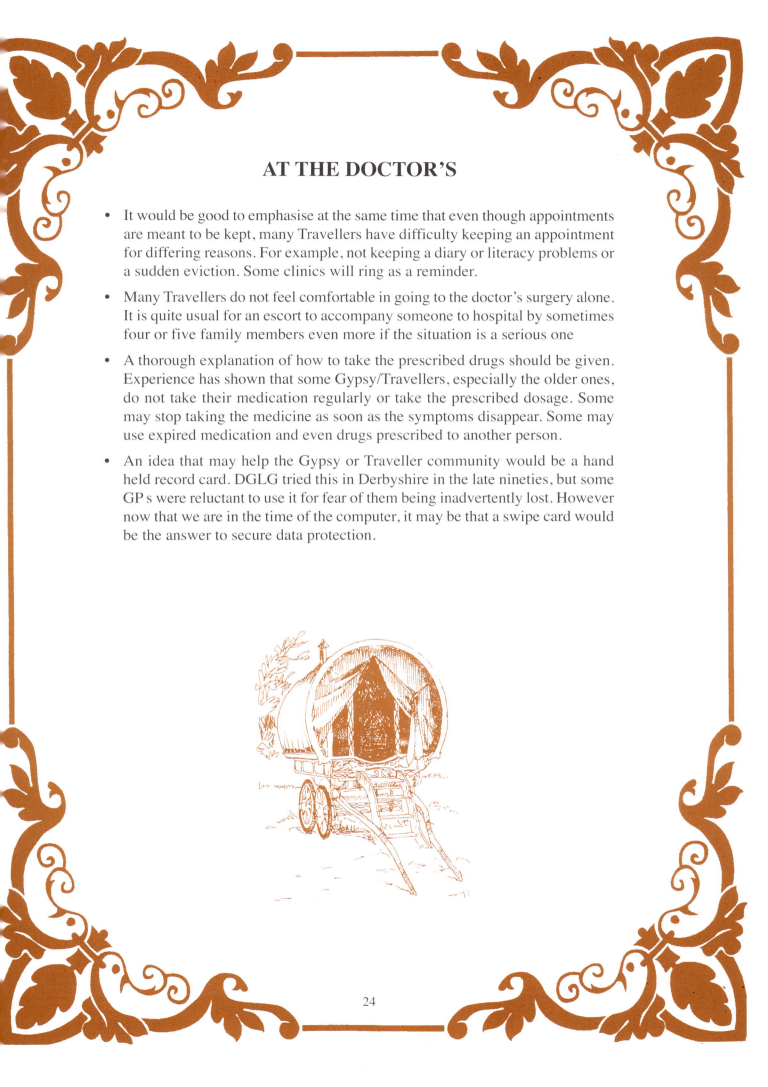

HOSPITAL SERVICES.

- Any patient can be afraid of medical procedures. Therefore it would be good practice to explain thoroughly to the patient exactly, what will be done, and why, before the actual operation.

- There is no medical treatment that Gypsy/Travellers would absolutely not accept.

- They should be told exactly and clearly how the treatment will proceed, what will be done and how the operation will be carried out and this will enable them to give an informed consent. The treatment should be explained and discussed before and after the operation.

- Post-operative care should be explained bearing in mind that there can be literacy problems. So it is best not to rely on handouts or advisory letters.

- In general, Gypsy or Traveller men do not care whether the doctor or carer is a man or a woman.

- For many Gypsy & Traveller women it is more comfortable if the doctor or carer is a woman.

- If the patient or a close relative wishes everybody to be present, the carer can do as he/she sees best. It would be advisable for the carer not to inquire about bodily functions in the presence of 'mixed company' (men and women).

- The bags used to collect excretion should if possible, be put where they cannot be seen.

- The covers should not be taken off the patient if other Gypsy Travellers are in the room.

- The examination and their results should be discussed separately with the patient.

- Intimate issues can be discussed freely in the presence of peers and members of the same sex.

- A child's condition and illness can be freely discussed with the child's parents.

- When the patient cannot move properly after the operation he/she should be helped in washing his/her hands before eating as Romany people wash their hands before they have anything to do with food or dishes.

- Medical instruments must not be put on the same table that the food is served on. For example bed pans and similar items.

DRESS

- Many Traditional Gypsy/Travellers are very shy and awkward about undressing in front of strangers.

- Showing some understanding of a patient's reluctance of undressing in front of, or by, strangers will help the patient to feel at home in the hospital.

- Some older Traveller patients may feel uncomfortable wearing hospital clothes or even sleeping in the hospital sheets. If the elder wishes the relatives to bring his/her own linen, it should be allowed as this could make the elder person feel more at home.

- When the patient is sufficiently recovered and is able to move and walk independently he/she should be allowed to wear his/her own day clothes - at least during the visiting hours, if it is in any way possible, as many of the community feel very embarrassed to be seen in their night wear.

- Privacy in dressing and undressing is very important.

- As an example in one hospital case there was an elderly Traveller man who refused to get undressed and get into bed, he preferred to sit in the chair that was by the bed, adamant that the 'hospital bed was for dying in'. This is not uncommon.

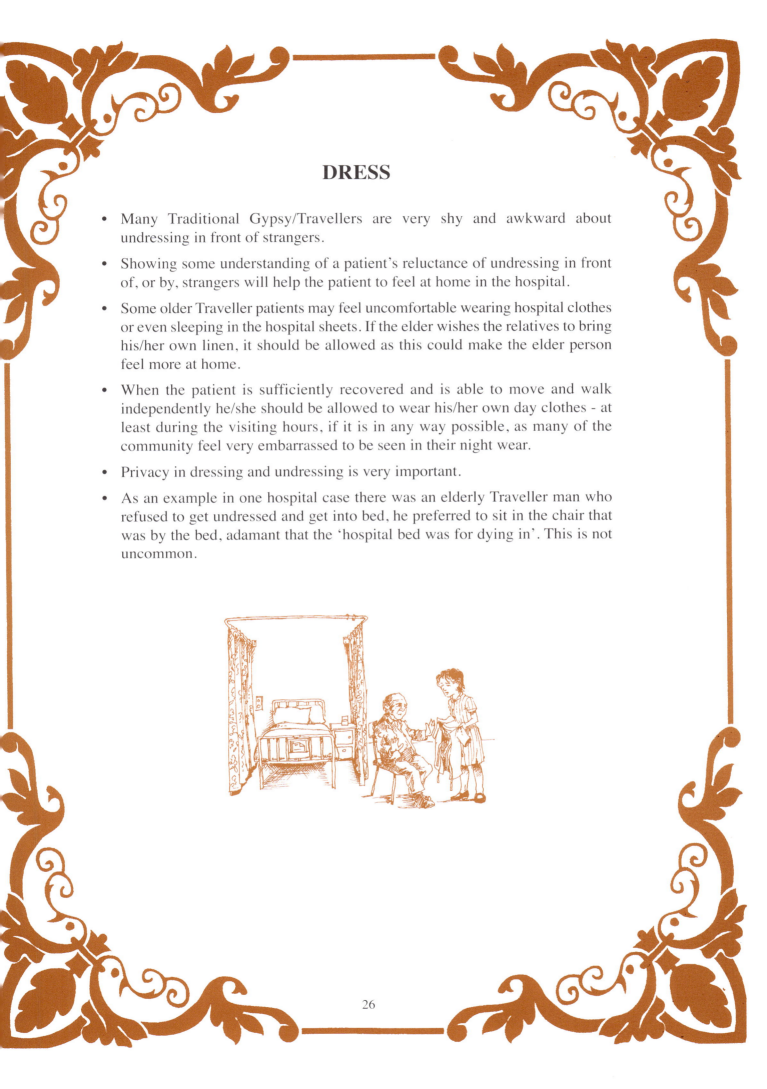

MEAL TIMES & FOOD

- It may seem that some members of the Gypsy community are being awkward when they refuse to eat hospital food. This it is due to the fact that many families, especially elders like to know where their food has been prepared and by whom. They are suspicious of outside catering.

- In some cases relatives have brought in home made food for the patient. In such cases it is important to be on the ball and make sure that the relatives have been informed of what kind of food is allowed, if the patient is on a special diet, or if an operation is about to take place

- In some hospitals Gypsy people have been allowed to use their own dishes and relatives have taken charge of cleaning up. If it makes the patient feel better then that is a good thing.

- There are no rules relating to what can or cannot be eaten in the traditional Gypsy/Traveller culture.

VISITS

- It is hospital policy to try and encourage close relatives to undertake caring responsibilities. Often, hospital staff can be amazed by the number of visitors a Gypsy or Traveller patient can receive. It is very important that family members be allowed access to their relative in the hospital

- Family and friends will come in large numbers to visit a sick person. If the situation is serious they will come from great distances, as they want to take care of the person and be with them in their time of need. This will make the patient feel much better as there is nothing worse for a person who is used to having many family members around them than, suddenly ending up isolated and alone.

- If a sick person grows tired, or if his/her condition deteriorates due to the visits, it is wise to use a close relative as a mediator and clarify the situation with him/her. The mediator can pass the medical staff's wishes to the other Traveller visitors. This can be done to ensure that the patient's room will not be crowded with too many people. There will be at least one close person that can allow discussions to be held.

- Gypsy/Travellers will come to the hospital even if they are not allowed to see the patient. They can be found in the corridors, in the restaurant, the cafe and the car park. This is their way of supporting their relatives and showing that they are worried or concerned about them. It is comforting for the relatives to be able to share with one another any worries caused by the illness.

- To stop other patients from being disturbed, if there is a single or double bay spare, it may be wiser to use that for the patient as family members will want to look after their relative's personal care themselves.

- If his/her room is near the entrance to the ward this will also help to alleviate too many people coming onto the ward at any one time.

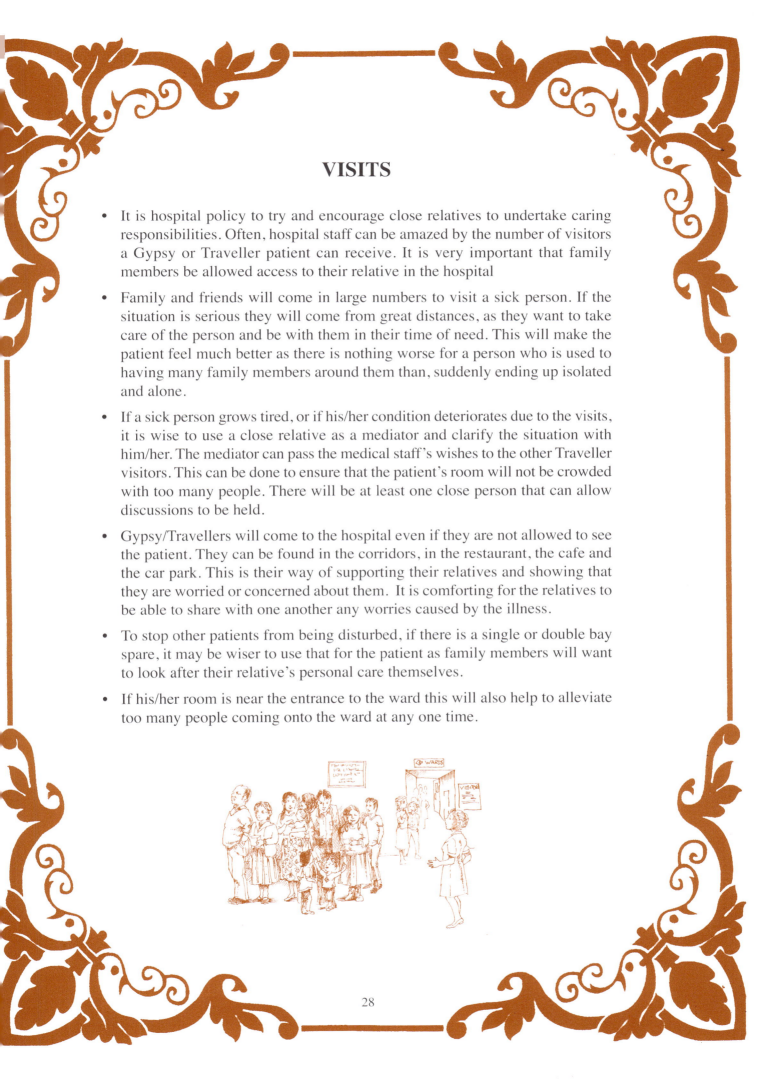

A DYING PATIENT

- For both the Romani Gypsy and Irish Travellers it is traditional to come from great distances to see a gravely ill person.

- The whole family takes part in the care of the dying relative. This will give the dying a feeling of security and reduce the trauma.

- The relatives are close by during the whole time the patient is in the hospital. It is usual for family to remain in the hospital all night and take turns to sit with the patient until morning.

- Immediately after the patient has died, a great number of relatives and friends can descend on the hospital to support the family.

- Many Gypsy/Travellers will come to the hospital also when the body is about to be put into the coffin.

- The hospital staff usually arrange for the undertaking service & the deceased will be clothed and then put into the coffin. Sometimes a close relative will want to take part in the clothing. The deceased best set of clothes is used. Some relatives will wait outside, others will come to the chapel of rest in the hospital, or to the deceased trailer depending on where the body has been laid out. Often a lighted candle is placed at the foot and the head of the deceased person. Traditionally while sitting up, white cloths such as cotton sheets are used to drape the coffin stand and the interior of the trailer. Some families will still ceremonially burn the caravan after the funeral. Failing this, it will be sold on.

GOING HOME

- Hospital care regarding recovery should be explained to the patient and his/her family, especially if the patient wants to leave the hospital before it is advisable. This has happened in the past, for example, when eviction was imminent and the families were concerned about leaving a relative in the hospital or just because the patient is not accustomed to being "imprisoned by four walls".

- It is important to thoroughly discuss the after-care when the patient is going home. It can be difficult for the patient to understand that he/she may not be in good shape for a long period of time after an illness or injury. Conversely, hospital staff do not always understand the implications of eviction on the recovery process or the difficulties that it can cause when trying to keep a follow-up appointment.

- Ideally the patient should be in the hospital a sufficient time to ensure complete recovery, although this is not always possible for a variety of reasons. Gypsy and Traveller people find it extremely difficult to be cooped up in doors

- Some patients might not understand advice and many will be illiterate. All care instructions and the prescription of medications should be explained clearly to the home-going patient. It is the custom now to release patients with a variety of information booklets, please bear in mind that many Gypsy people cannot read these. Remember to ring to remind of after care appointments.

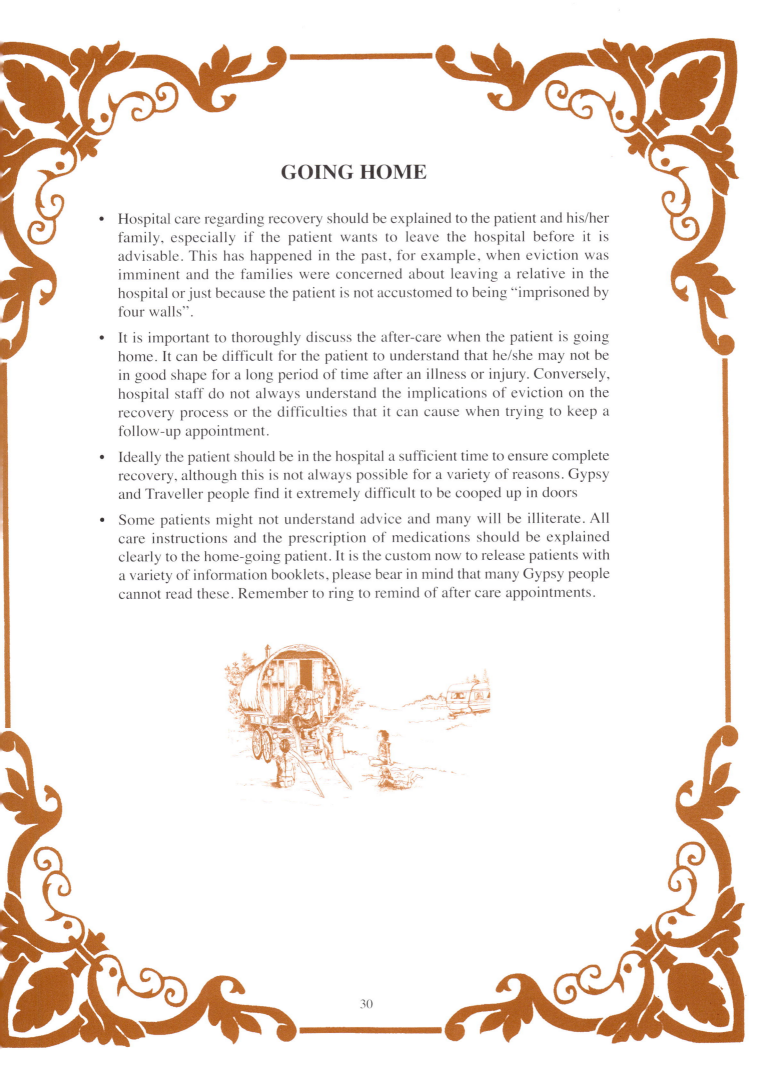

RESOURCES

Useful Websites

Derbyshire Gypsy Liaison Group works on various issues accommodation, education, health promotional materials, it works locally, regionally and nationally
www.dglg.org

Teachers Aids /educational books to aid literacy/
www.robertdawson.co.uk

Networking of the Regions. The Federation keep the GTLRU meetings going with Lord Avebury to work on Gypsy & Traveller Law Reform
www.nationalgypsytravellerfederation.org

British Gypsy and Traveller History website
www.rtfhs.org.uk

UK Magazine for Gypsies and Travellers
www.travellerstimes.org.uk

Gypsy and Traveller Law Chris Johnson

(CLP Travellers advice Team)
www.blog.travellerstimes.org.uk/gypsy-and-traveller-law/

The Patrin Web Journal: Romani Culture and History
www.geocities.com/~patrin/

Footnotes

[i] 9th of March 2005 the Sun newspaper launched its Stamp on the camps campaign
http://www.thesun.co.uk/sol/homepage/news/article104007.ece

[ii] Daily Express article 17th November 2008, headlined Families must sell land for Gypsy Campsites, www.travelerslaw.0rg.uk. January 2009 newsletter No7.

[iii] *The Race Relations Act 1976, and Race Relations (Amendment) Act 2000*. This Act places a duty on public authorities, including local authorities, to eliminate unlawful discrimination and promote equal opportunities and good race relations. The Act requires local authorities to assess the impact of any proposed policies on all ethnic minorities; and to have due regard to the need to eliminate unlawful racial discrimination, to promote equality of opportunity and good relations between persons of different racial groups. Gypsies were recognised as an ethnic minority in 1989, and Irish Travellers in 2000.

October 2008 Scottish Gypsies are a distinct ethnic group for purposes of the Race Relations Act of 1976. Judge Nicol Hosie overturned the decision of a previous hearing in March 2008. This gives Scottish Gypsies the same protection under the 1976 Act.

The Human Rights Act 1998 This Act came into effect in October 2000 when provisions of the European Convention on Human Rights were incorporated into UK law. The Act makes it unlawful for a public authority to act in breach on Convention Rights unless it could not have acted differently under primary legislation. Any interference with a Convention Right must be proportionate to the objective in question and must not be arbitrary, unfair or oppressive.

[iv] *Treaty Series No. 42 (1998) Framework Convention for the Protection of National Minorities*
Strasbourg, 1st February 1995[The United Kingdom instrument of ratification was deposited on 15 January 1998 and the Convention entered into force for the United Kingdom on 1st May